How good are you at finding the clitoris? See how many clitorises (*clitori?*) you can find hidden in this spread.

W9-AWW-122

^{the}clitourist

a guide to one of the hottest spots on earth

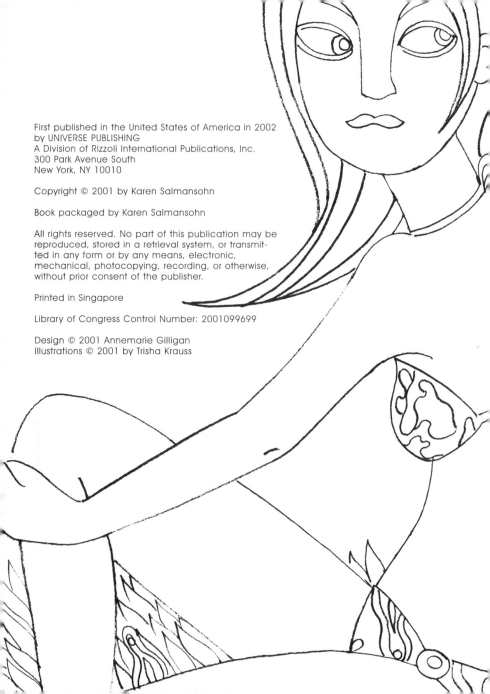

First published in the United States of America in 2002
by UNIVERSE PUBLISHING
A Division of Rizzoli International Publications, Inc.
300 Park Avenue South
New York, NY 10010

Book packaged by Karen Salmansohn

Printed in Singapore

Library of Congress Control Number: 2001099699

Design © 2001 Annemarie Gilligan
Illustrations © 2001 by Trisha Krauss

the
clitourist

Written by **Karen Salmansohn**
Illustrated by **Trisha Krauss**
Designed by **Annemarie Gilligan**

chapter 1

Penis envy, p'Shaw.

Bush

It's funny how well people know and understand the penis and its many quirks —what it looks like, where to find it, how to feed it and make it happy—yet so little is known about the clitoris. This goes for not only lay people *(pardon the entendre),* but professionals, too.

According to Jennifer Berman, one of the nation's few female urologists: "If you look in any anatomical text there are twenty pages on the male sexual anatomy and two pages on the female. And there are conflicting reports as to how one should describe the female anatomy."

Yes, even at the beginning of the 21st century, there is still a pathetic lack of information available on the clitoris. What information we women do have we owe to a scientist named Kermit Krantz. Back in the 1950s, Krantz first discovered the many wonders of this tiny nether region while dissecting women's corpses.

To his surprise, Kermit observed an extremely high concentration of nerve endings packed into this one

teeny weeny spot—the highest concentration of nerve endings on the entire female body—which Kermit wisely deduced would make this spot the most sensitive on a woman's body.

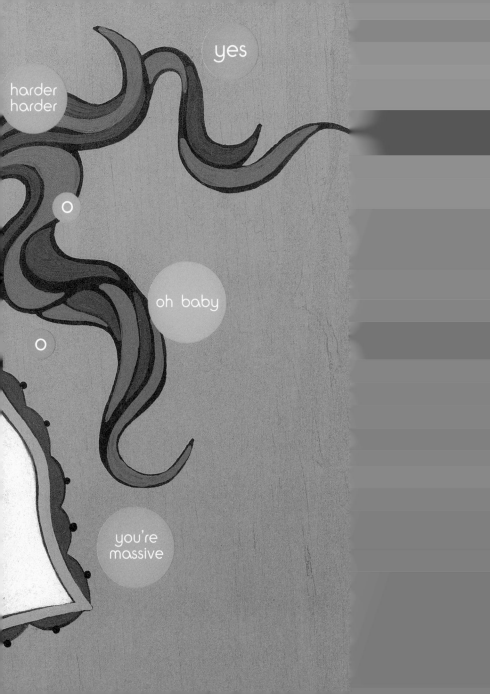

"Thanks, Kermie."

The discovery of these tiny nerve endings marked the beginning of

a huge change in women's **sex lives**—and

their skin complexions—soon after, as well.

"Freud, you're so wrong...."

Before Kermit came along, we were a vaginally centered culture. Freud had advertised the vagina as the #1 place to go for an orgasm and spread bad PR rumors about women who could not have vaginal orgasms—claiming these women had defective egos.

Thanks to Kermit, Freud's theories were later proven to be defective.

Eventually, the clitoris began to get the credit it justly deserved, and is on its way to becoming a part of our everyday common vocabulary —although many of us, including myself, still do not know for sure how to pronounce the word.

cli

toris

rhymes with Delores

or..

clit-

or

is

rhymes with spit on this?

Clitoris is one of those words like
vase that has two pronunciations.
Vase = "VaHs" or "vAIze"

Vase

Vas

The clitoris is hands-down a girl's Primary Pleasure Center—and it is the only organ found in either man or woman that exists for pleasure alone. Many biologists believe that for this very reason, women's genitals are more evolved than men's. However, the clitoris also has much in common with a man's genitalia, offering up the same goods—but with more nerve endings and entertainment options.

When Kermit first discovered the clitoris, he even described it as a **"mini penis,"** because he noted how it, too, consisted of a head *(glans)* and a body *(shaft)*—except with the clitoris, the glans is only visible to the highly curious eye.

And finally, analogously to the penis, the

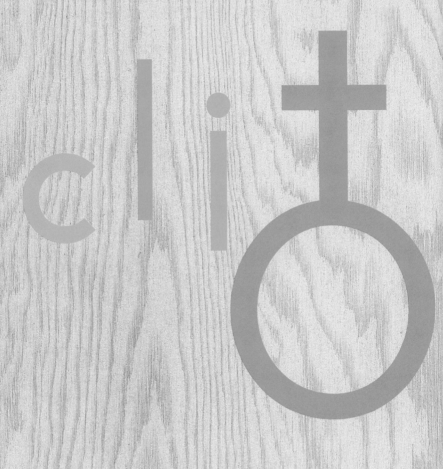

riS

is made of tissue that **swells** during sexual arousal.

At first these similarities led to the belief that the clitoris should be "operated" like a penis. So men began to rub at it—which, well, proved to be rather, er, um, uncomfortable.

But, hey, I don't mean to complain. These men meant well. Plus, it wasn't just men who were confused as to what was going on down there. We women also could not see the

buSh f o r e s t for the

Some of us still don't know our way around this mysterious bushland.

Well, I say, as Socrates recommended, "Know thyself, girlfriend!"

Coming up in the pages ahead, you'll find everything you need to know about the clitoris—for the people who have one, or for the people who love people who have one.

chapter 2

Everything you need to know to know your way
around, UM, ER...

...down there

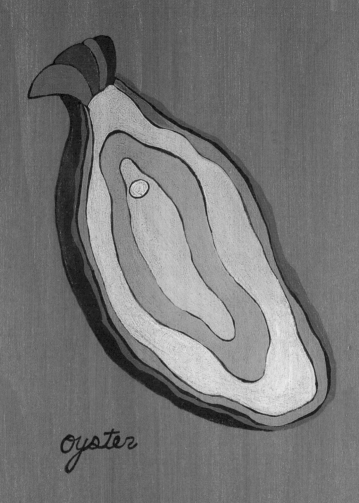

oyster

It's funny how most of us can label every inch of a man's genitalia, but don't know a woman's vulva from her vagina.

At least—I must confess—I did not.

Yes, it was surprising for me—not only the author of this book, but the owner of a vagina for all my life—to learn that what I originally thought was "my vagina" was actually "my vulva," and vice vulva versa.

The vulva, I've come to learn, is what represents the entire little chia pet of an area resting between a woman's legs. The vagina is just one area of the vulva—specifically the entry zone for...

...Sex.

In other words: vulva is to face what vagina is to nose.

Then there are all the other assorted metaphorical eyebrows and chins and mustaches floating around down there that I—in-my-post-vulva-epiphany—realized I still needed to study up on.

So, I did.

And now I'm ready to pass on to you my newly charted and quite helpful map of the vulva so we can put an end to this female genitalia paraphernalia confusion once and for all.

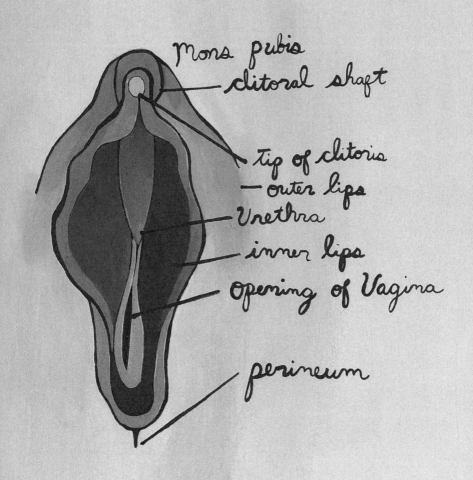

Mons pubis
clitoral shaft

tip of clitoris
outer lips
Urethra
inner lips
Opening of Vagina

perineum

georgia O'Keeffe's Vulva

Mons pubis: The fleshy mound that sits atop the pubic bone. This spot, though often vastly ignored, is a major turn-on zone worthy of exploration.

The clitoris: tip, glans, and hood.

Outer lips or Labia Majora: Ironically named, since these lips are often smaller than the Labia Minora. You can tell the two apart *(or rather, four apart)* because these are the one with the hairdo.

The urethral opening: aka the pee hole.

Inner lips or the Labia Minora: These are the big, fat bald guys, and like a lot of big, fat, bald guys you know, they have loads of personality. They tend to do lots of talking to the clitoris during intercourse. So if you get in good with them, they'll tell the clitoris wonderful things about you.

The vagina: The main entry for the heterosexual entrée: intercourse.

The perineum: Also a secret sexual turn-on zone.

As you can see from this illustration, the clitoris is located a good inch away from the vagina—and it's a very good inch to go hunting around in.

Like the penis, the clitOris has a variety of looks and personalities. They are as individual to each woman as her thumbprint. Some clitorises are very sensitive. Some are not sensitive at all. SOme pop out immediately. Others are a bit mOre shy about making their presence known.

And the clitOris can range a lOt in size: anywhere from two to twenty millimeters in diameter. HumOrously, whereas many a man has believed his penis tO be bigger than it is, we wOmen, it seems, have been underestimating our clitOris size.

Researchers now believe the clitOris to be bigger than originally deemed.

According to sOme new theories, the clitOris is even being measured tO include the wishbone structure around it, including the legs of the wishbOne underneath each of the labia—making it humongOus.

no. no.

yes.

maybe.

no.

no.

yes. yes.

maybe.

maybe. it depends,

no.

no.

yes.

maybe

it depends,

yes*

*keep it coming, baby.

OK, now you've located your clitoris. So what the heck do you do with it, you may be wondering.

Well, first of all, it's important to keep in mind that no two women's clitorises work exactly the same way—and no one woman gets turned on exactly the same way twice.

A woman's genital sensitivities can change depending upon the time of month, or time of day, or whether or not she really wants to give the person she's with the time of day.

Yes, we girls are indeed complicated creatures. Because of this, when it comes to dealing with the clitoris, I recommend keeping in mind an old Buddhist proverb: "In the beginner's mind there are many possibilities. In the expert's mind there are few."

In other words, although it's important to learn everything you can about that special little clitoris in your life—it's also important to forget all you learn each time you meet up with your clitoris, because each time it will be in an entirely different kind of mood.

So, be sure to suss out your clitoral mood up front—tired, friendly, **ready to party**—then proceed appropriately with one of the following

5 CLITORIS APPROACHES:

The Manual Approach
The Oral Approach
The Penile Approach
The H2ohoh Approach
The R2D2 Approach

chapter 3

The manual approach
(for two people or less)

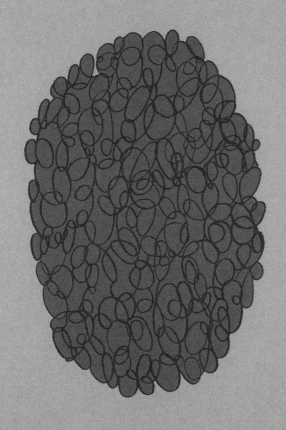

Brillo

...get a mirror, and check out what it is you like to busy yourself with down there.

Did you know that more people *Masturbate* than perform nearly any other sexual activity? So, don't feel bad about learning to make yourself feel good. Instead...

Do you fancy direct contact with the clitoris—or do you prefer a more indirect communication system? If so, what other spots do you play favorites with? What spots have you yet to fully explore? Have you researched the full benefits of pressure on the *Mons pubis* area—the place just above where your lips meet?

Or maybe you prefer some playful *petting* in neighboring regions?

Are you *pro lubrication*—or do you prefer to go no-lubrication? What types of touch do you prefer: hard, soft, fast, slow?

Do you benefit from the ol' Tug-on-*Nipple* Ripple Effect?

HOW TO BECOME A SHOW GIRL

Use your partner's finger to point to what it is you like.
Or simply have your partner watch you and your clitoris
getting chummy. Or if you have time on your hands, turn
your hands into the hands of a watch to be watched.
Envision a watch face on your clitoris, then rock around
the clock. Start at the high noon position. Then try the 1
o'clock position. Then 2 o'clock. Then 3 o'clock. Keep
rocking around the clock until you find the spot and
rhythm that rocks your world.

Keep in mind: Different Folks Like Different Strokes. And don't keep this info to yourself. Share what you discover with someone you love.

If you feel it's too naughty to talk about all this clitoral stuff out loud, then become a "SHOW GIRL."

chapter 4

The oral approach

papaya

1. a shaver

2. shaving cream

SHAV
CREA

3. a pillow

If you're open to exploring a little,
um, er, how shall I put it...
"talking in tongues,"
then check out the three sexual
aids on the opposite page.

Both sexual aid #1 and sexual aid
#2 should be used not only by
you, but also your partner.

If your partner is male, he should
shave himself, so he doesn't
give you razor burn.

And you *(or your partner, dare I suggest)*
should then shave your little chia
pet zone, for better viewing access.

Lastly, there's sexual aid #3.
Prop yourself atop a pillow, for
even better viewing access.

Once
you've
taken
your
place
upon
that
pillow
pedestal,
your
partner
should
take
his or her
place
facing
you
while
on
his or her
stomach.
He or she
should
then
crawl
closer
and
closer
to
you,
like
a
scuba
diver
**swimming
toward**
a
sunken
treasure
trove—
which

of
course
this
little
precious
zone
of
yours
is.

Finally,
your
partner
should
approach
your
clitoris
with
an
intentionally
bad
sense
of
direction.
Just
as
he
or she
gets
close
to
the
intended
destination,
he
or she
should
promptly
get
lost
again.

BE A CT TO A SE

l.tOris

YOUR PARTNER'S #2 GOAL: After sufficient teasing, pay attention to the clitoris, its every little need and whim.

YOUR PARNER'S NEW #1 FEAR: Uh-oh. Where did she put that clitoris of hers again? I can't seem to find it. It appears to have vanished into this newly swelling area.

(NOTE: When it comes to the clitoris, what feels swell will swell. As a woman gets more aroused, the vulva will swell, and the clitoris itself will get lost in all the excitement.)

YOUR PARTNER'S NEW AND #1 SOLUTION FOR THIS FEAR:

Make an educated guess as to where that lil' clitoris could be hiding, and keep on seeking it. Or see TIP #1 FOR THE TIP OF YOUR PARTNER'S TONGUE, below.

TIP #1 FOR THE TIP OF YOUR PARTNER'S TONGUE:
Lick slowly from the vagina to the top of the vulva.

Somewhere along the way will be a little speed bump–aka the clitoris. What follows thereafter is up to you–though do check out TIP#2 FOR THE TIP OF YOUR PARTNER'S TONGUE.

TIP #2 FOR THE TIP OF YOUR PARTNER'S TONGUE: Learn everything there is to know about that clitoris from a to z, literally and cliterally. Try writing the alphabet with your tongue on your paramour's clitoris, until she finds a letter she really (*really*) likes.

Then try writing the alphabet all over again in cursive—or Sanskrit. Or try humming the national anthem down there, or your favorite *NSYNC song.

SOME ADDED LIP SERVICE: During all of the above, check out a little labia tugging action.

SOME ADDED PRO-BONO WORK: Also try some pushing on the ol' pubic bone area.

A WARNING: There is such a concept as "too much of a good thing." The clitoris, like the penis, can get overly sensitive if overstimulated. Let your partner's response guide you.

chapter 5

The penile approach

Beaver

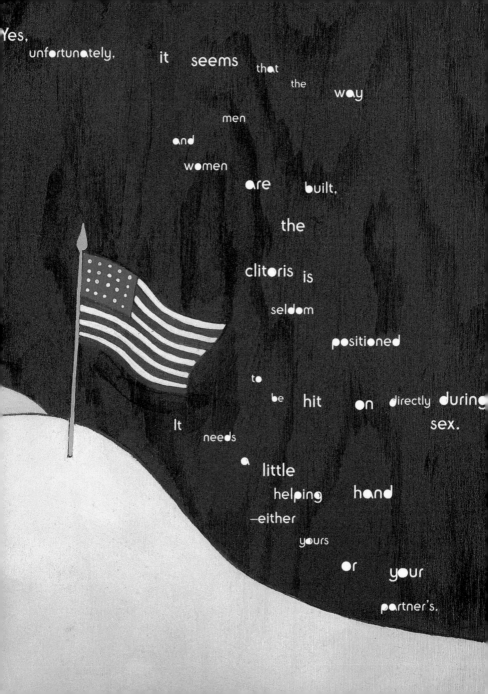

Yes, unfortunately, it seems that the way men and women are built, the clitoris is seldom positioned to be hit on directly during sex. It needs a little helping hand —either yours or your partner's.

After your partner has made his grand theatrical entrance, it's advisable that a friendly finger or two, yours or your partner's, remain behind at the entrance, not only to keep in contact with the clitoris, but also to do some lip reading with the Labia Minora—aka the inner lips.

The inner lips, and not the outer ones, are the more important lips to pay attention to during intercourse. A good way to remember this is to think: intercourse...innercourse...intercourse...innercourse...intercourse ...innercourse...intercourse.

The inner lips naturally get pushed back and forth a lot during sex—

and these are the lips known for loving to talk to the clitoris in the first place. So the more you can get these inner lips talking, the better. Another way to get in good favor with your clitoris is to watch how you straighten and bend your legs during sex. When your legs are straight during sex, penetration is not as deep, but the clitoris gets more stimulation.

The
H2Ohoh
approach

Pussy

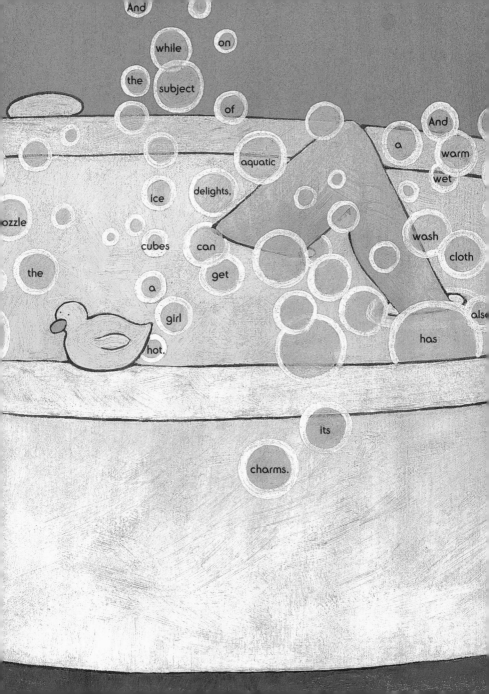

The
R2D2
approach

cotton
candy

When it comes to **orgasms,** sometimes there's nothing like a little technological help in the form of **a vibrator.** Interestingly enough, the vibrator was first intended to be used in a *(get ready to gasp)* doctor's office. It was invented in the early 1800s by Doctor Joseph Mortimer Granville and was originally used exclusively by doctors as a medical device to cure women of any and all **psychological instabilities** and **neuroses.** Back in the 1800s, doctors were very quick to diagnose women to be suffering from all sorts of psychological problems, or what they termed

"hysteria."

And doctors were just as quick to prescribe a vibrator as the cure-all, explaining how this device created what they called a **"hysterical paroxysm."**
(And I suppose that means that at times women would experience "multiple hysterical paroxysms.")

ANYWAY...these doctors back in the early 1800s were big fans of the vibrator, believing this machine could help move female patients through their offices more speedily than the *(get ready to gasp yet again)* manual method of inducing hysterical paroxysm—which had already been a popular treatment for women for a decade or so.

ACTUALLY...it took a while for the vibrator to ever leave the confines of the doctor's office and enter the bedroom *(or kitchen, or what have you)*, because the earliest vibrators were steam powered. Yes, you had to keep shoveling coal into the engine to keep the thing going.

ULTIMATELY...not only has the medical profession discovered that vibrators and/or masturbation are not the most appropriate medical treatments for women's psychological problems, but technology has also since determined that battery power beats the bupkiss out of steam power.

"The Wabbit"

"The loverboy"

Thankfully
there are now a
plentiful and whimsical
array of battery pow-
ered vibrators available
for home use.

And there's one in
particular, with little bunny
rabbit ears at its base, that
many of my friends confidentially
promote as being one of the most
clitoris friendly in the US of
A-and beyond.

"The Napoleon"

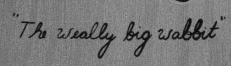

"The weally big wabbit"

chapter 8

Trouble shooting

It's interesting how our culture has the expression "blue balls" to describe when a man ultimately does not achieve orgasm, but we don't have an expression like

" Blue Labia,"

to describe when a lady doesn't get to climax—which can happen waaay too often either because: (1) A lady may feel it's not ladylike to indulge in her truest and most urgent sexual desires, so she stops herself from continuing with her favorite sexual shenanigans. Or (2) A gal just turns plain ol' frigid from sexual guilt and shame.

It's unfortunate we don't talk more about "blue labia"—a term I'm making up, and eager to pass on—because I feel this subject should become a more familiar part of our sexual vernacular and thereby more easily discussed.

I also feel "blue labia" is a highly apt term because it truly describes what happens to the opposite of an orgasmic labia, which is the following...

THE LIFE AND TIMES OF AN ORGASMIC LABIA:

The more aroused a woman gets, the redder her labia becomes.

They receive tremendous blood flow, not only engorging them in size, but also reddening them in color.

Biologists believe this reddening is nature's way of saying to any nearby guy: "Hey, lookie over here, fella! Pay attention to this glowing red area!"

When a mate does indeed follow nature's orders, a female orgasm is likely to ensue—and last anywhere from one to ten seconds, and repeat itself two to three times before the labia returns to its natural size and color.

It's hard to describe the feeling of an orgasm. Though if you imagine **fireworks + shoe shopping** you wouldn't be too far off.

A female orgasm is available in two varieties:

1. The g-spot orgasm

2. The clitoral orgasm*

Both orgasms are not only experienced differently as far as sensation goes, but they are also biologically quite different.

It's like this:

The clitoris is connected to the pudendal nerve. The g-spot is connected to the pelvic nerve. As a result, the clitoral orgasm travels to the brain via a different path. Interestingly, women with spinal cord injuries still have clitoral orgasms because these orgasms travel a different route than the g-spot orgasm.

*Or just call it the "gee-whiz spot" orgasm.

AN A-Z DESCRIPTION OF G-SPOT ORGASMS:

A is for "A FINGER" which is needed to explore the roof area of the vagina until it finds a little rough spot.

A NOTE TO WATCH YOUR PEES AND CUES: Some women feel a bladder-type fullness when aroused this way. And some women purposefully do not pee for a while before sex to help enhance this kind of orgasm.

Z is for "ZIGZAG MOTIONS" which the finger makes on this spot: a "come hither" motion that, done right, can—bingo—bring about g-spot orgasms.

chapter 9

A secret The
Sexual
organ

orchideae clitoreae

Many psychologists and sex therapists agree: if you've applied the appropriate strategies for clitoral orgasm and g-spot orgasm—and are unhappily greeted by blue labia—chances are the problem lies in your mind and not your body.

Psychologists and sex therapists have described blue labia in official terms as:

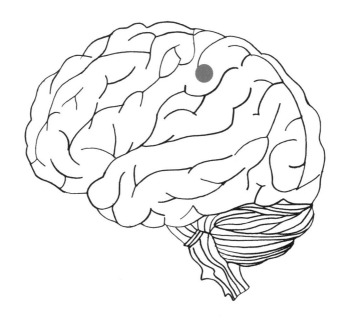

Sexual Arousal Disorder
Orgasmic Disorder muffled
Orgasmic Disorder
Hypoactive Sexual Disorder

Many of these disorders have been known to overlap and be caused by or accompanied by depression or other emotional problems.

In other words, the mind and body are in cahoots.

if you wanna get on your body's good side, you gotta find out what's troubling your mind.

Were you scolded as a child for touching yourself? As a child were you made to feel Sex is shameful? were you sexually abused as a child? Are you angry with yourself for something?

You must get to the root of your buried problem — then pull this buried problem out by its roots..... so hopefully it won't grow back into a problem again... and again.... and again.

chapter 10

To fake or
Not to Fake

fig

Many philosophers have pondered the following question: should a woman fake orgasm?

When you think about it, faking orgasm IS a white lie. Men tell women those too—only in other areas. A man might deceive a woman by saying: "Gee, honey, you look thin when you're angry." Or "No, honey, your new haircut doesn't make you look like a squirrel."

In fact, a man's lie about a bad haircut is exactly like a woman's faked orgasm. The man knows a bad haircut is a temporary disadvantage of sorts.

Eventually hair grows longer again. Likewise, a woman knows when it comes to problems in bed, if given time, certain things will...er...um...also grow longer again...and she can perhaps have a better...er..um...experience when this thing does grow back long again.

You know what I mean?

But alas, in the end, I CANNOT advocate faking.

I believe a girl should be honest with her partner about orgasm for the following reasons:

1. Let's say your orgasm problem is your partner's technique problem. You could be potentially aiding and abetting in mis-educating someone about how to satisfy a woman—and thereby not only spoiling things for yourself, but for the rest of womankind, who—after you and your mis-educated partner break up, most likely due to your repressed sexual resentment—will suffer under his or her mis-educated techniques. *(Boo-hiss on YOU!)*

2. Forget the above. Let's say your partner is doing everything 100% right, yet you're still not experiencing "fireworks + shoe shopping." Well, if you feel you're physically healthy, your blue labia problem most likely means a blue mood problem—and could be a sign that you have bigger issues to address. Meaning? It's worth it to face up to your sexual problems with your partner so together you can potentially figure out not only how to achieve **SEXUAL SATISFACTION** but **LIFE SATISFACTION.** Together you and your partner can—and should—spend time exploring not just your **EROTIC ZONES**...but your **NEUROTIC ZONES**—and figure out what might be troubling you on a deeper level.

3. Being honest about lack of orgasm means you're being a vulnerable and honest communicator—always a plus in a relationship.

4. Although I am against a woman faking orgasm, I am not against a woman faking **NOT HAVING HAD** an orgasm, thereby encouraging her partner to keep going and going...and going...and going. *(Uh, that was a joke. Really.)*

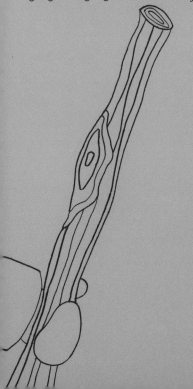

chapter II

Care and
upkeep

fur burger

Some women—and those who love them—appreciate a good pubic hairdo as much as a good public hairdo—though it depends on the gal what this hairdo may be.

Some like a muff with scruff—some like it more whiskerfree—others yet prefer it as bald as a Sphinx cat (*the hairless pet of preference for Austin Powers*).

So first pick a "do" that's right for you...then pick your favorite

HAIR TODAY, GONE TOMORROW PROCEDURES:
Shaving
Depilatories
Waxing
Brazilian waxing

"The Farrah Fawcett"

"The George W"

Each of these have PROS (*i.e. long lasting effects*) and CONS (*i.e. high intensity pain*) —and some can be done by pros to lessen the cons.

For instance, if you're into waxing, salons are the least painful/longest lasting choice for giving your mysterious Bermuda Triangle a Brazilian—where every nook and cranny gets waxed and waned away. So if you're not a talented stripper, just let a salon take it off—take it all off, baby—for you.

Okay. That's the inside story on the outside story of upkeep.

Now, here's the inside story on what goes on on (ahem) the inside, just a few centimeters away from the clitoris itself.

Meaning: should a girl buy lots of fancy shmancy perfumey shpritzy douchey products? In most cases: no. The vagina is a natural self-cleaning machine.

"The Vagina"

"The Andy Warhol"

Your standard soap and washcloth should keep things in odor order.

Ironically, many feminine perfumeries sold can actually increase odor because they get things stirred-up down there that should be settling-down instead.

And be aware, if you douche more than three times monthly, you have three times the chance of getting pelvic inflammatory disease (not a pretty thing).

Okay. That about covers everything. Oh—except for how to cover everything. Finally, let's talk about repacking your merchandise in some nice lacy lingerie, shall we. But first, let's check out that word lingerie. Note how it has the word LINGER hidden inside of it.

And when you are hidden inside of LINGERie then often some very fun LINGERING can take place. And even some CUNNILINGERING.

Okay, NOW that truly covers everything there is to know about clitorises—in both the literal sense—and clitoral sense.

I hope that you use the information within this book to improve your sex life—which should soon help to improve your emotional and spiritual life, as well. I even suggest you read the book together with your partner—as a happy bedtime story—a story that I hope will have an extremely happy bedtime ending.

And if you have any questions, please feel free to write me c/o Universe Publishing. But hopefully you will be MUCH too busy to write.

Have fun! Gotta go! See you labia!

about the author

Karen Salmansohn is the bestselling author of **How To Make Your Man Behave in 21 Days or Less Using the Secrets of Professional Dog Trainers**, and **How To Be Happy, Dammit: the cynic's guide to spiritual happiness**—plus many other books with equally feisty titles.